A Cozy
QUILTED CHRISTMAS

90 Designs, 17 Projects to Decorate Your Home

Kim Schaefer

C&T PUBLISHING

Text © 2007 Kim Schaefer

Artwork © 2007 C&T Publishing, Inc.

Publisher: Amy Marson

Editorial Director: Gailen Runge

Acquisitions Editor: Jan Grigsby

Editor: Lynn Koolish

Technical Editors: Helen Frost and Ellen Pahl

Copyeditor/Proofreader: Wordfirm Inc.

Cover Designer: Kristen Yenche

Design Director/Book Designer: Kristen Yenche

Illustrator: Tim Manibusan

Production Coordinators: Kerry Graham, Matt Allen

Photography: Luke Mulks and Diane Pedersen unless otherwise noted

Front cover: Photography by Diane Pedersen, props from Grangewood Antiques

Location sets and props: Margaret Peters

Published by C&T Publishing, Inc., P.O. Box 1456, Lafayette, CA 94549

ISBN 978-0-7394-8425-8

Printed in China

This is a book club edition.

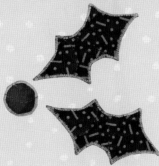

Dedication

To my family, who make the holidays and life worth celebrating.

Acknowledgments

Thanks to:

My dad, Jerry Sanders; my mom, Alice Sanders; and my sisters, Jill Sanders Trachte and Kelly Sanders. Thank you for the memories and traditions of a lifetime of Christmases spent together.

My husband, Gary Schaefer, who after twenty years of wedded bliss still manages to be supportive, encouraging, and somewhat patient with me. I'm just so glad I picked you over all the other boys. Thank you for transcribing my handwritten mess to disk for this book.

Lynn Helmke, my favorite longarm quilter, for your beautiful work and for always meeting and exceeding my demanding deadlines.

Andover/Makower Fabrics for the generous supply of fabric, much of which was used in this book.

All at C & T Publishing: Thanks to Lynn Koolish, my editor. Thank you Lynn, for your expertise and for making the work on this book so easy. A very special thank you goes to Helen Frost, my technical editor. Helen painstakingly checks and rechecks all of my math for accuracy, it is a huge job and I am grateful to have someone so competent and easy to work with. Thank you to the very talented and creative Kristen Yenche for the great cover and book design. Finally, thank you to Tim Manibusan for the fine illustrations.

Contents

Introduction

Christmas is a magical time of year, filled with warm memories and honored traditions. Some of my fondest childhood Christmas memories include baking cookies with my mom and sisters, decorating the tree, and taking our customary after-dinner drive on Christmas Eve to look for Santa. Mom always stayed home to do the dishes on those memorable nights, and every year while we were out singing Christmas carols in the car, Santa would visit our house, and we'd miss him again.

Of all the Christmas rituals, one that continues to bring me joy is that of making handmade gifts to give to family and friends. In this book you will find a variety of Christmas projects suitable for all different skill levels. The festive table runners, coasters, towels, and wall and lap quilts are sure to become part of your holiday traditions and will help you to decorate and celebrate this holiday season. Some projects are simple—perfect for gift giving—while others will become cherished heirlooms to hand down for future generations to enjoy for years to come.

It is my hope that this collection of projects will inspire you to create some timeless treasures for the season and that the spirit of Christmas will be with you and your family throughout the year.

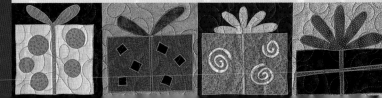

General Instructions

Rotary Cutting

I recommend that you cut all fabrics used in the pieced blocks, borders, and bindings with a rotary cutter, acrylic ruler, and mat. Trim the blocks and borders with these tools as well.

Piecing

All piecing measurements include ¼" seam allowances. If you sew an accurate ¼" seam, you will have happiness, joy, and success in quilting. If you don't, you will have misery, tears, and the ripper.

> **Tip** Many aspects of quilting don't require exact perfection for a folk look: matching plaids, choosing fabrics in a scrap quilt, or cutting the appliqué pieces. My biggest and best quiltmaking tip is to learn to sew an accurate ¼" seam.

Pressing

Press the seams to one side, preferably toward the darker color. Press flat, and avoid sliding the iron over the pieces, which can distort and stretch them. To join 2 seamed sections, press the seams in opposite directions. Doing so makes it much easier to nest and match the seamlines, and it reduces bulk.

Appliqué

All appliqué instructions are for fusible web with machine appliqué. If you prefer a different appliqué method, you will need to add seam allowances to the appliqué pieces.

Appliqué pieces have been drawn in reverse. A lightweight fusible web works best for machine appliqué. Choose your favorite, and follow the manufacturer's directions.

In general:

1. Trace all parts of the appliqué design to the paper side of the fusible web. Trace each layer of the design separately. Usually the bottom layer of the design is cut as 1 piece, and the detail pieces are added on top. Add the pattern letter and/or number to each traced shape.

2. Cut loosely around the appliqué shapes, leaving a ¼" margin around each piece.

3. Press and fuse the shapes to the *wrong* side of the fabric. Cut on the traced lines, except where a piece extends under an adjacent piece. Leave ⅛" to ¼" beyond the line on these edges. Peel off the paper backing from the appliqué web. A thin web will remain on the wrong side of the fabric, which will adhere the appliqué pieces to the backgrounds.

4. Position the pieces on the backgrounds. Press, and fuse in place.

5. Machine stitch around the appliqué shapes using a zigzag, satin, or blanket stitch. Stitch any other lines on the patterns to add detail.

My personal choice is the satin stitch. I use beige thread for all the stitching. Sometimes the stitches blend with the fabric, and sometimes they don't. Using 1 color throughout gives the quilt a folk art look.

Note: Appliqué numbers are for identification, not appliqué order.

Half-Square Triangles

Some of the projects use half-square triangle blocks (see *Holiday House* on page 19). Because the quilts are scrappy, I usually cut the triangles from squares and sew them individually. I always make more than I need so that I have choices when assembling the quilt top. In each project I give the exact measurements used in that quilt. If you want to change the size of the blocks, it is important to know the

basic formula for making half-square triangles: the finished size plus ⅞″. If you need a 6″ finished block, for example, cut the squares 6⅞″ × 6⅞″. Cut the squares in half diagonally to make 2 triangles. I refer to this as "cut the square on the diagonal."

Putting It All Together

When you have completed all the blocks for a quilt, lay them out on the floor or, if you're lucky enough to have one, a design wall. Arrange and rearrange until you are happy with the overall look of the quilt. This step is especially important in scrap quilting. Each project has specific directions for assembling the top. Refer to the diagrams and photos.

Borders

All borders in the book are straight cut with no mitered corners. This technique renders a more folk look, and it's easier and faster, too. Join together strips at a 45° angle, as necessary, to achieve the desired length.

Layering the Quilt

Cut the batting and backing pieces 2″ to 3″ larger than the quilt top for runners and smaller quilts (less than 40″) and 3″ to 4″ larger on each side than the quilt top for larger quilts. Lay the pressed backing on the bottom, with the right side facing down. Place the batting over the backing and the quilt top on top. Make sure that everything is flat and smooth and that the quilt top is centered over the batting and backing. Pin or baste the quilt.

Quilting

Quilting your top is a personal choice; you may prefer hand or machine quilting. My favorite is to send the quilt top to a longarm quilter. This method keeps my number of unfinished quilt tops low and finished quilts high.

Color and Fabric Choices

Many books cover the subject of color theory, addressing terms such as *analogous, secondary, complementary, primary, tonal value,* and *color range.* In choosing fabric, you will hear terms such as *scale, contrast, value,* and *balance.* I have a more relaxed approach to color and fabric choice. If I like it, I use it. Scrap quilting lends itself well to this approach. Generally, the more fabrics I use, the more I like the quilt. Everyone has different tastes. In the end it's your quilt and your choice, and if you're happy, that's what's important.

Making the Quilt Your Own

It is my hope that you will use the projects in this book as inspiration and a starting point to make your own quilts. If you want to change the size of a quilt, simply add or subtract blocks or change the width of the borders. Feel free to mix and match the designs. You can also enlarge or reduce the appliqué patterns at your local copy shop. Your color choices may be totally different from mine.

Yardage and Fabric Requirements

I have given yardage and fabric requirements for each project, with many calling for a "total" amount of assorted fabrics for use as a base for your quilt. The yardage amounts may vary depending on several factors: the size of the quilt, the number of fabrics used, and the number of pieces you cut from each. I don't worry about running out of a particular fabric; with a scrappy look this isn't a factor.

I prefer to use the lengthwise grain of the fabric for quilt backings, even on smaller projects. For larger quilts, I piece together 2 or 3 lengths of fabric.

Binding fabric amounts allow for 2″-wide strips cut on the straight of grain. Fusible web amounts are based on a 17″ width.

Photo by Sharon Risedorph

Dress up the holidays with this elegant, yet casual, poinsettia quilt. The traditional color combination of red and green is paired with tans and golds that add warmth and richness to make this quilt a classic favorite. *Quilted by Lynn Helmke*

Finished Block Size: 10″ × 10″

Finished Lap Quilt: 64½″ × 84½″

❄ Materials

2⅛ yards light gold textured solid for appliqué block backgrounds

1½ yards total assorted tans and golds for pieced blocks and flower centers

2½ yards total assorted greens for pieced blocks

1½ yards total assorted reds for poinsettias

⅝ yard red for inner border

1½ yards black print for outer border

5¾ yards for backing and binding

3½ yards of paper-backed fusible web

❄ Cutting

❄ Cut 17 squares 10½″ × 10½″ from the light gold textured solid for the appliqué block backgrounds.

❄ Cut 72 squares 3″ × 3″ from the assorted tans and golds for the pieced blocks.

❄ Cut 72 squares 3⅜″ × 3⅜″ from the assorted tans and golds for the pieced blocks. Cut the squares on the diagonal for a total of 144 triangles.

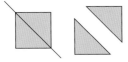

Cut squares on diagonal.

❄ Cut 144 squares 3⅜″ × 3⅜″ from the assorted greens for the pieced blocks. Cut the squares on the diagonal for a total of 288 triangles.

❄ Cut 68 squares 3″ × 3″ from the assorted greens for the appliqué blocks.

❄ Pieced Blocks

1. Sew 144 triangles from the assorted tans and golds to 144 triangles from the assorted greens. Press toward the greens.

Make 144.

2. Sew 72 triangles from the assorted greens to 72 triangles from the assorted greens. Press.

Make 72.

3. Make 18 pieced blocks.

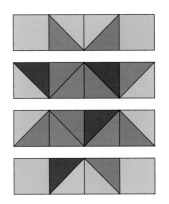

Block assembly

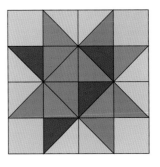

Make 18.

❄ Appliqué Blocks

1. To make the appliqué block backgrounds, mark a diagonal line on the wrong side of the 3″ assorted green squares. Place them on the corners of the 10½″ light gold squares. Sew on the marked lines. Trim the excess fabric.

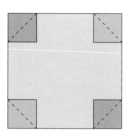 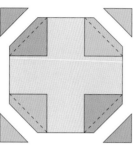

Sew on lines.   *Trim excess fabric.*

2. Press the seams toward the green triangles.

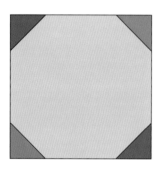

Make 17.

3. Cut the poinsettia appliqué pieces (the patterns are on Pullout 1, Side B, at the back of the book). Cut 17 each of Patterns 1 through 13, and 51 of Pattern 14.

4. Appliqué the appropriate pieces onto the blocks. Make each block unique by varying the way the petals overlap each other.

Make 17.

❄ Putting It All Together

Refer to the diagram below.

Blocks

Arrange and sew the blocks in 7 rows of 5 blocks each. Sew together the rows. Press.

Borders

Inner Border

1. From the red fabric, piece and cut 2 strips 2″ × 70½″ for the side borders. Sew the borders to the quilt top, and press toward the borders.

2. Piece and cut 2 strips 2″ × 53½″ for the top and bottom borders. Sew the borders to the quilt top, and press toward the borders.

Outer Border

1. From the black print, piece and cut 2 strips 6″ × 73½″ for the side borders. Sew the borders to the quilt top, and press toward the borders.

2. Piece and cut 2 strips 6″ × 64½″ for the top and bottom borders. Sew the borders to the quilt top, and press toward the borders.

Finishing

1. Layer the quilt top with batting and backing, and baste or pin.

2. Quilt as desired, and bind.

Putting it all together

All Wrapped Up Lap Quilt

 This holiday season, wrap yourself or someone you love in this lap quilt featuring wrapped presents set off by red and white pieced blocks. *Quilted by Lynn Helmke*

Finished Block Size: 8″ × 8″

Finished Lap Quilt: 64½″ × 80½″

❄ Materials

3½ yards total assorted reds for appliqué block backgrounds, pieced blocks, and presents

3½ yards total assorted lights for appliqué block backgrounds, pieced blocks, and presents

2¼ yards deep red for border

5½ yards for backing and binding

5 yards of paper-backed fusible web

❄ Cutting

❄ Cut 14 squares 8½″ × 8½″ from the assorted reds for the appliqué block backgrounds.

❄ Cut 10 squares 8½″ × 8½″ from the assorted lights for the appliqué block backgrounds.

❄ Cut 146 rectangles 2½″ × 4½″ from the assorted reds for the pieced blocks.

❄ Cut 166 rectangles 2½″ × 4½″ from the assorted lights for the pieced blocks.

❄ Pieced Blocks

Sew 8 rectangles together to make a pieced block. Make a total of 39 blocks.

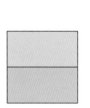

Step 1   *Step 2*

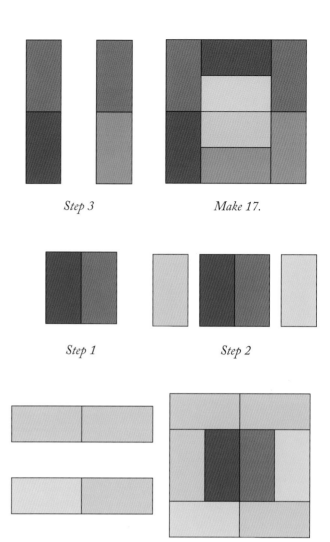

Step 3   *Make 17.*

Step 1   *Step 2*

Step 3   *Make 22.*

❄ Appliqué Blocks

1. Cut 4 each of the present appliqué pieces (the patterns are on Pullout 1, Side A, at the back of the book).

2. Appliqué the appropriate pieces onto each block. Place circles, stars, and swirls as desired.

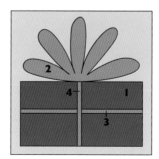

Block A, make 4.

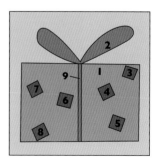

Block B, make 4.

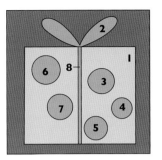

Block C, make 4.

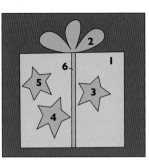

Block D, make 4.

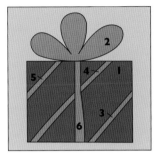

Block E, make 4.

Block F, make 4.

❄ Putting It All Together

Refer to the diagram at right.

BLOCKS

Arrange and sew the pieced blocks in 7 rows of 5 blocks each. Sew together the rows to form the pieced block section of the quilt top. Press.

BORDERS

Appliqué Block Border

1. Sew together 2 rows of 5 appliqué blocks for the top and bottom borders. Add a pieced block on each end of the appliqué block rows. Press.

2. Sew together 2 rows of 7 appliqué blocks for the side borders. Press.

3. Sew the side borders to the quilt top. Press toward the borders. Sew the top and bottom borders to the quilt top. Press toward the borders.

Outer Border

1. From the deep red fabric, cut 2 strips $4\frac{1}{2}'' \times 72\frac{1}{2}''$ for the side borders. Sew the borders to the quilt top, and press toward the borders.

2. Cut 2 strips $4\frac{1}{2}'' \times 64\frac{1}{2}''$ for the top and bottom borders. Sew the borders to the quilt top, and press toward the borders.

FINISHING

1. Layer the quilt top with batting and backing, and baste or pin.

2. Quilt as desired, and bind.

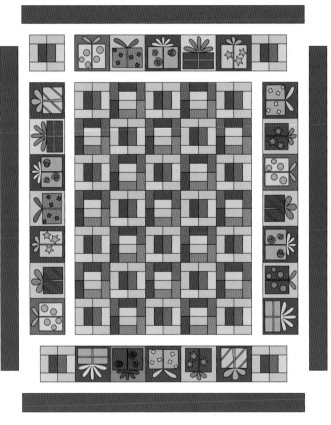

Putting it all together

Stripes and Holly Berry Vines Lap Quilt

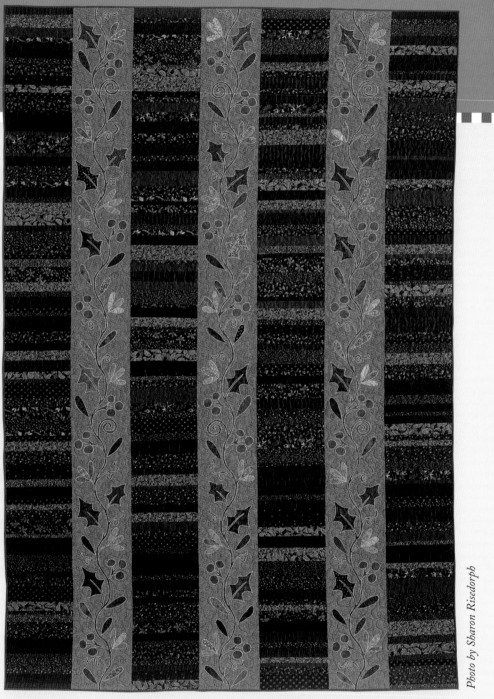

Randomly pieced stripes offset appliquéd holly berry vines for a simple, yet sophisticated, look. Shades of black and gray lend an old-fashioned feeling to this quilt. *Quilted by Lynn Helmke*

Finished Block Size: 9″ × 9″

Finished Lap Quilt: 60½″ × 90½″

❄ Materials

2¾ yards gray for appliqué background

4 yards total assorted Christmas prints with black backgrounds for pieced blocks

2⅝ yards green for vines

1 yard total assorted greens for holly and leaves

¼ yard red for berries

6 yards for backing and binding

5 yards of paper-backed fusible web

❄ Cutting

❄ Cut 3 pieces 8½″ × 90½″ from the gray for the appliqué block backgrounds.

❄ From the assorted black prints for the pieced blocks:

Cut 80 rectangles 1¾″ × 9½″.

Cut 80 rectangles 1¼″ × 9½″.

Cut 40 rectangles 2½″ × 9½″.

Cut 40 rectangles 1″ × 9½″.

Cut 40 rectangles 2″ × 9½″.

Cut 40 rectangles 1½″ × 9½″.

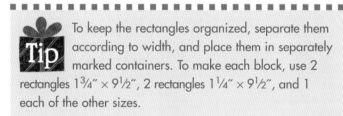

To keep the rectangles organized, separate them according to width, and place them in separately marked containers. To make each block, use 2 rectangles 1¾″ × 9½″, 2 rectangles 1¼″ × 9½″, and 1 each of the other sizes.

❄ Pieced Blocks

1. Sew together the following rectangles in random order to make a pieced block:

1″ × 9½″ rectangle (1)

1¼″ × 9½″ rectangle (2)

1½″ × 9½″ rectangle (1)

1¾″ × 9½″ rectangle (2)

2″ × 9½″ rectangle (1)

2½″ × 9½″ rectangle (1)

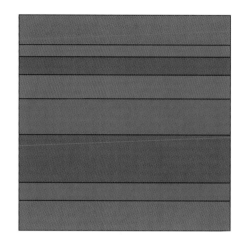

Make 40.

The blocks will look different because they are sewn in random order, but each block will measure 9½″ × 9½″. Refer to the diagram on page 14.

2. Sew together the blocks in 4 rows of 10 blocks each. Press flat.

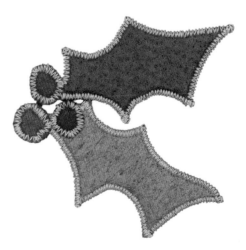

❄ Appliqué

1. Use the holly and berry vine patterns (the patterns are on Pullout 1, Side B, at the back of the book) to cut:

- ❊ 4 each of Patterns 1, 2, and 6 through 27
- ❊ 16 each of Patterns 3, 4, and 5
- ❊ 2 of Pattern 28
- ❊ 2 each reverse of Patterns 1, 2, and 6 through 27
- ❊ 8 each reverse of Patterns 3, 4, and 5
- ❊ 1 reverse of Pattern 28

2. Appliqué the appropriate pieces onto the background pieces, using the diagrams at right.

❄ Putting It All Together

Refer to the diagram below.

BLOCKS

Sew together the rows, alternating pieced block rows and appliqué pieces. Press flat.

FINISHING

1. Layer the quilt top with batting and backing, and baste or pin.

2. Quilt as desired, and bind.

Make 2.   Make 1.

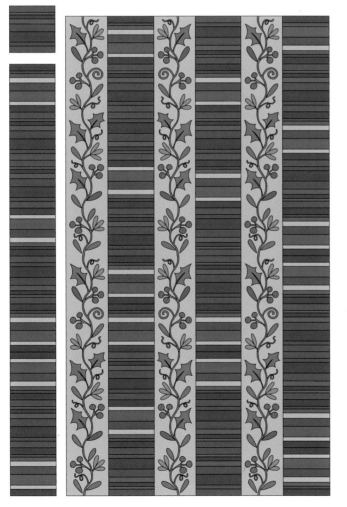

Putting it all together

Log Cabin Trees Lap Quilt

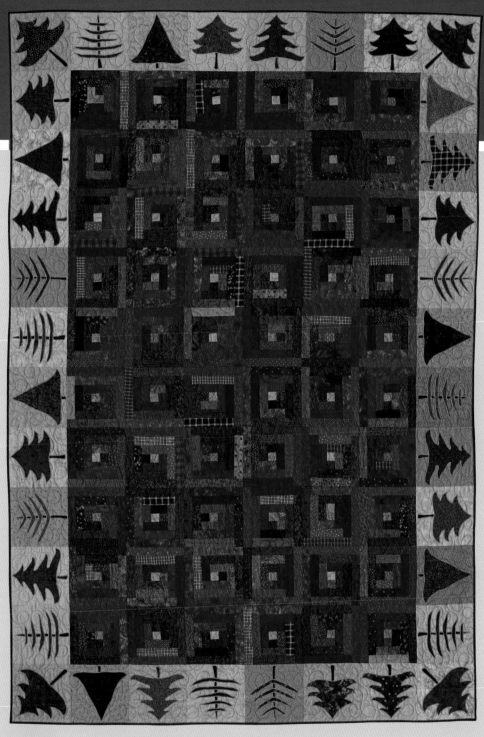

Cuddle up under this lap quilt through the holidays and all winter long. Traditional Log Cabin blocks are framed by a border of appliquéd trees. *Quilted by Lynn Helmke*

Finished Block Size: 7″ × 7″

Finished Lap Quilt: 56½″ × 84½″

❄ Materials

2¼ yards total assorted golds and tans for appliquéd block backgrounds and pieced blocks

3½ yards total assorted greens for pieced blocks and trees

2½ yards total assorted reds for pieced blocks

¼ yard total assorted browns for tree trunks

5¾ yards for backing and binding

3½ yards of paper-backed fusible web

❄ Cutting

❄ From the assorted golds and tans:

Cut 36 squares 7½″ × 7½″ for the appliqué block backgrounds.

Cut 60 squares 1½″ × 1½″ for the pieced blocks.

❄ From the assorted greens for the pieced blocks:

Cut 60 squares 1½″ × 1½″.

Cut 60 rectangles 1½″ × 2½″.

Cut 60 rectangles 1½″ × 3½″.

Cut 60 rectangles 1½″ × 4½″.

Cut 60 rectangles 1½″ × 5½″.

Cut 60 rectangles 1½″ × 6½″.

❄ From the assorted reds for the pieced blocks:

Cut 60 rectangles 1½″ × 2½″.

Cut 60 rectangles 1½″ × 3½″.

Cut 60 rectangles 1½″ × 4½″.

Cut 60 rectangles 1½″ × 5½″.

Cut 60 rectangles 1½″ × 6½″.

Cut 60 rectangles 1½″ × 7½″.

❄ Pieced Blocks

Piece the Log Cabin blocks, and press flat after each addition. Make 60 blocks.

Step 1

Step 2

Step 3

Step 4

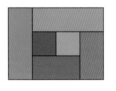

Step 5

Step 6

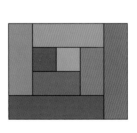

Step 7

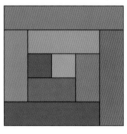

Step 8

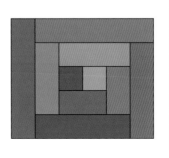

Step 9

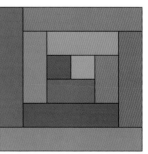

Step 10

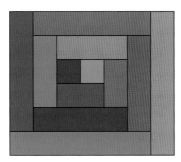

Step 11

Block B, make 6.

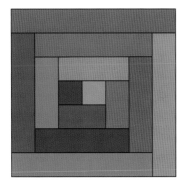

Step 12

Piece blocks, make 60.

Block C, make 7.

❄ Appliqué Blocks

1. Cut the tree appliqué pieces (the patterns are on Pullout 3, Side A, at the back of the book).

2. Appliqué the appropriate pieces onto each block.

Block A, make 4 for corner blocks.

Block D, make 5.

Block E, make 7.

Block F, make 7.

❄ Putting It All Together

Refer to the diagram at right.

BLOCKS

1. Arrange and sew the Log Cabin blocks in 10 rows of 6 blocks each. Press flat.

2. Sew together the rows to form the pieced block section of the quilt top.

APPLIQUÉ BORDER

1. Sew together 2 rows of 10 appliqué blocks for the side borders. Sew the borders to the quilt top. Press toward the borders.

2. Sew together 2 rows of 8 appliqué blocks for the top and bottom borders. Sew the borders to the top and bottom of the quilt top. Press toward the borders.

FINISHING

1. Layer the quilt top with batting and backing, and baste or pin.

2. Quilt as desired, and bind.

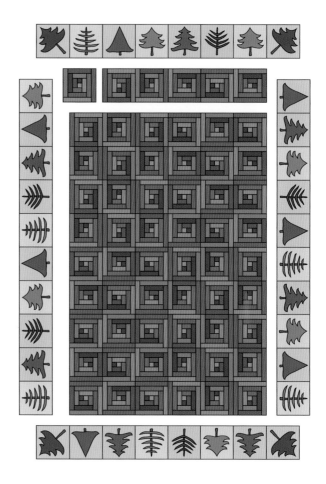

Putting it all together

Holiday House Wall Quilt

The holiday house is the center of attraction in this folksy and fun wall quilt. This quilt glows with the rich, warm colors of the season.

Quilted by Lynn Helmke

Finished Wall Quilt: 44½" × 44½"

❄ Materials

2 yards total assorted tans and golds for appliqué block backgrounds and presents, ornaments, star, candle holders, and flames

¾ yard total assorted lights for appliqué block backgrounds and house, presents, and candles

¼ yard black for windows, stars, holly berry vine, smoke, and ornament string

1½ yards total assorted greens for trees, holly leaves, ornament, star, wreath, scallops, and pieced border

1½ yards total assorted reds for roof, chimney, door, stars, ornament, berries, bow, and pieced border

1⅓ yards dark green for outer border

3 yards for backing and binding

3½ yards of paper-backed fusible web

❄ Cutting

❋ Cut 1 rectangle 12½″ × 16½″ from gold for the house block background.

❋ Cut 1 rectangle 6½″ × 16½″ from tan for the large tree block background.

❋ Cut 4 rectangles 5″ × 4½″ from the assorted tans for the ornament background.

❋ Cut 1 rectangle 4½″ × 26½″ from gold for the holly and berries background.

❋ Cut 7 squares 4½″ × 4½″ from the assorted golds for the star block backgrounds.

❋ Cut 5 rectangles 6½″ × 7½″ from the assorted golds for the scallop backgrounds.

❋ From the assorted tans for the present block backgrounds:

Cut 1 rectangle 5½″ × 8½″.

Cut 1 square 5½″ × 5½″.

Cut 1 rectangle 5½″ × 6½″.

Cut 1 rectangle 5½″ × 7½″.

Cut 1 rectangle 5½″ × 9½″.

❋ Cut 7 squares 5½″ × 5½″ from the assorted golds for the tree block backgrounds.

❋ Cut 10 squares 2½″ × 2½″ from the assorted greens for the checkered border section.

❋ Cut 10 squares 2½″ × 2½″ from the assorted reds for the checkered border section.

❋ From the assorted greens for the side pieced border:

Cut 3 rectangles 2½″ × 4½″.

Cut 3 rectangles 3½″ × 4½″.

Cut 1 rectangle 1½″ × 4½″.

Cut 1 square 4½″ × 4½″.

❋ From the assorted reds for the pieced border:

Cut 1 rectangle 1½″ × 26½″.

Cut 2 rectangles 2″ × 26½″.

❋ Cut 8 squares 5⅞″ × 5⅞″ from the assorted reds for the pieced border. Cut the squares on the diagonal for a total of 16.

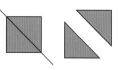

Cut on diagonal.

❄ Appliqué Blocks

1. Cut the appliqué pieces (the patterns are on Pullout 2, Side A, at the back of the book). For the house (Piece 4), cut 1 piece 8″ × 9″. For the holly vine, cut 1 piece ¼″ × 25″.

2. Sew together in a row 4 rectangles 5″ × 4½″ for the ornament block backgrounds. Press. Appliqué the appropriate pieces onto the backgrounds.

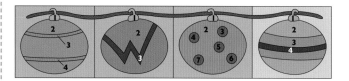

Ornament blocks, make 1.

3. Appliqué the appropriate pieces onto each block.

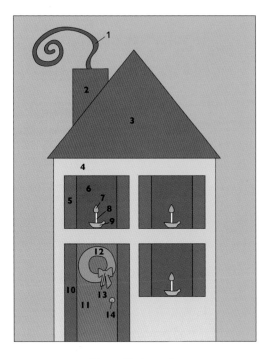

House block, make 1.

Large tree block, make 1.

Holly berry block, make 1.

Star block, make 7.

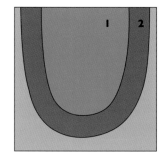

Scallop block, make 5.

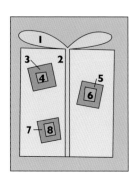

Present block A, make 1.

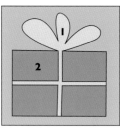

Present block B, make 1.

Present block C, make 1.

Present block D, make 1.

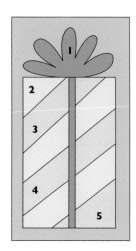

Present block E, make 1.

Tree block A, make 2.

Tree block B, make 2.

Tree block C, make 2.

Tree block D, make 1.

❄ Putting It All Together

Refer to the diagram at right.

BLOCKS

1. Sew together the 7 star blocks in a row.

2. Sew together the 5 scallop blocks in a row.

3. Sew together the 5 present blocks in a row.

4. Sew together the 7 tree blocks in a row.

BORDERS

Pieced Borders

1. Sew together 2 rows of 10 squares from the assorted reds and greens to form the checkered border section. Press.

Sew checkered border section.

2. Sew together the side pieced border section from the assorted green fabrics. Press.

Sew green border section.

3. Sew together the pieced border section from the assorted red fabrics. Press.

Sew red border section.

4. Sew 8 light red triangles to 8 deep red triangles on the diagonal edge to form squares. Sew 8 squares together in a row for the pieced border section. Press.

Sew pieced triangle section.

5. Assemble the appliqué blocks and pieced borders. Press.

Outer Border

1. From the dark green fabric, cut 2 strips 2½″ × 40½″ for the side borders. Sew the borders to the quilt top, and press toward the borders.

2. Cut 2 strips 2½″ × 44½″ for the top and bottom borders. Sew the borders to the quilt top, and press toward the borders.

FINISHING

1. Layer the quilt top with batting and backing, and baste or pin.

2. Quilt as desired, and bind.

Putting it all together

Angels Wall Quilt

Let the angels watch over you this holiday season. This wall quilt features basic piecing techniques along with fusible appliqué. It's a great quilt to use your scraps. *Quilted by Lynn Helmke*

Finished Block Size: 12″ × 12″

Finished Wall Quilt: 48½″ × 48½″

❄ Materials

⅓ yard each 9 assorted lights for appliqué backgrounds and pieced blocks

2½ yards total assorted darks for pieced blocks and appliqué pieces

½ yard total assorted golds for angel wings

⅓ yard tan for faces, arms, and legs

1¼ yards gold for inner border

1½ yards navy for outer border

3⅓ yards for backing and binding

3 yards of paper-backed fusible web

Black and red permanent markers for faces and hair

❄ Cutting

❄ Cut 9 squares 8½″ × 8½″ from the assorted lights for the appliqué backgrounds.

❄ Cut 36 squares 2⅞″ × 2⅞″ from the assorted lights for the pieced blocks. Cut squares on the diagonal for a total of 72 triangles.

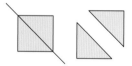

Cut on diagonal.

❄ Cut 108 squares 2½″ × 2½″ from the assorted darks for the pieced blocks.

❄ Cut 36 squares 2⅞″ × 2⅞″ from the assorted darks for the pieced blocks. Cut squares on the diagonal for a total of 72 triangles.

❄ Pieced Blocks

1. Sew 72 light triangles to 72 dark triangles on the diagonal edge. Press toward the dark triangles.

Make 72.

2. Piece the blocks as shown. Press.

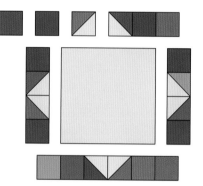

Block assembly.

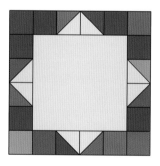

Piece block, make 9.

❄ Appliqué Blocks

1. Cut the angel appliqué pieces (the patterns are on Pullout 2, Side B, at the back of the book). Cut 9 each of Patterns 1 and 2. Cut 1 each of all other patterns.

2. Appliqué the appropriate pieces onto each block.

3. Use permanent markers to draw the angels' faces.

Block C, make 1.

Block A, make 1.

Block D, make 1.

Block B, make 1.

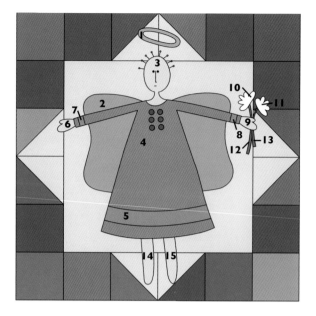

Block E, make 1.

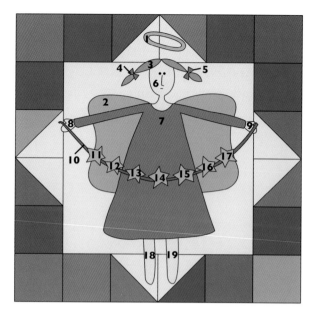

Block G, make 1.

Block F, make 1.

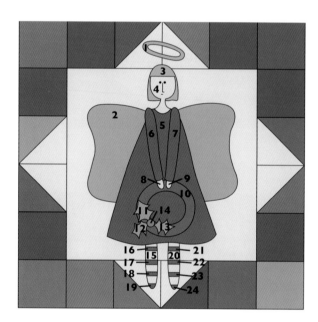

Block H, make 1.

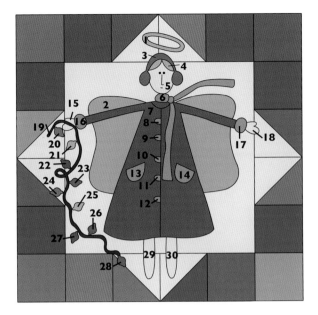

Block I, make 1.

❄ Putting It All Together

Refer to the diagram below.

BLOCKS

Arrange and sew the blocks together in 3 rows of 3 blocks each. Join the rows. Press.

BORDERS

Inner Border

1. From the gold fabric, cut 2 strips 2½″ × 36½″ for the 2 side borders. Sew the borders to the quilt top, and press toward the borders.

2. Cut 2 strips 2½″ × 40½″ for the top and bottom borders. Sew the borders to the quilt top, and press toward the borders.

Outer Border

1. From the navy fabric, cut 2 strips 4½″ × 40½″ for the 2 side borders. Sew the borders to the quilt top, and press toward the borders.

2. Cut 2 strips 4½″ × 48½″ for the top and bottom borders. Sew the borders to the quilt top, and press toward the borders.

FINISHING

1. Layer the quilt top with batting and backing, and baste or pin.

2. Quilt as desired, and bind.

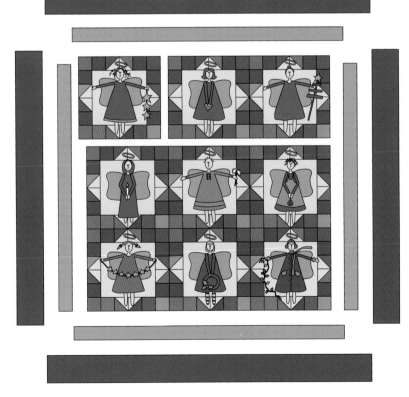

Putting it all together

Folksy, yet sophisticated, this quilt will lend a classy touch to your holiday decorating. Potted poinsettias are framed by Courthouse Steps blocks (a variation of the Log Cabin block) and scrappy square side borders. *Quilted by Lynn Helmke.*

Finished Wall Quilt: 29½″ × 36½″

❄ Materials

¾ yard tan for appliqué background

⅛ yard gold for centers of pieced blocks and poinsettia centers

1 yard total assorted reds for pieced blocks and poinsettias

1¼ yard total assorted greens for pieced blocks, stems, leaves, and pieced side borders

⅓ yard light for pot

⅛ yard light for berries

1½ yards for backing and binding

1 yard of paper-backed fusible web

❄ Cutting

❋ Cut 1 rectangle 21½″ × 19½″ from the tan for the appliqué block background.

❋ Cut 6 rectangles 1½″ × 2″ from the gold for the pieced blocks.

❋ From the assorted greens for the pieced blocks:

Cut 6 rectangles 1½″ × 2″.

Cut 6 rectangles 1½″ × 5″.

Cut 6 rectangles 1½″ × 3½″.

Cut 6 rectangles 1½″ × 7″.

Cut 6 rectangles 1½″ × 5½″.

Cut 6 rectangles 1½″ × 9″.

❋ From the assorted reds for the pieced blocks:

Cut 6 rectangles 1½″ × 2″.

Cut 6 rectangles 1½″ × 5″.

Cut 6 rectangles 1½″ × 3½″.

Cut 6 rectangles 1½″ × 7″.

Cut 6 rectangles 1½″ × 5½″.

Cut 6 rectangles 1½″ × 9″.

❋ Cut 72 squares 2½″ × 2½″ from the assorted greens for the pieced side borders.

❄ Pieced Blocks

1. Piece the 6 Courthouse Steps blocks. Press after each strip is added to the block.

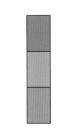
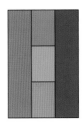

Step 1   *Step 2*

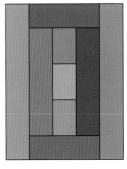

Step 3   *Step 4*

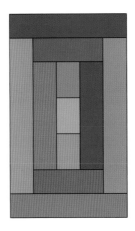
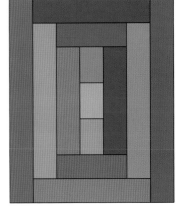

Step 5   *Step 6, make 6.*

2. Sew 2 rows of 3 blocks each. Press.

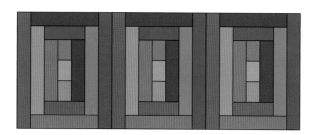

Make 2.

✳ Appliqué Block

1. Cut the poinsettia and pot appliqué pieces (the patterns are on Pullout 3, Side A, at the back of the book).

2. Appliqué the appropriate pieces onto the background.

Appliqué center block.

✳ Putting It All Together

Refer to the diagram below.

BORDERS

Sew together 2 rows of 18 green squares for the side borders. Make 2 borders.

BLOCKS AND BORDER

1. Sew the rows of pieced blocks to the appliqué block. Press toward the pieced blocks.

2. Sew the pieced side borders to the quilt top. Press toward the borders.

FINISHING

1. Layer the quilt top with batting and backing, and baste or pin.

2. Quilt as desired, and bind.

Putting it all together

O Christmas Tree
Wall Quilt

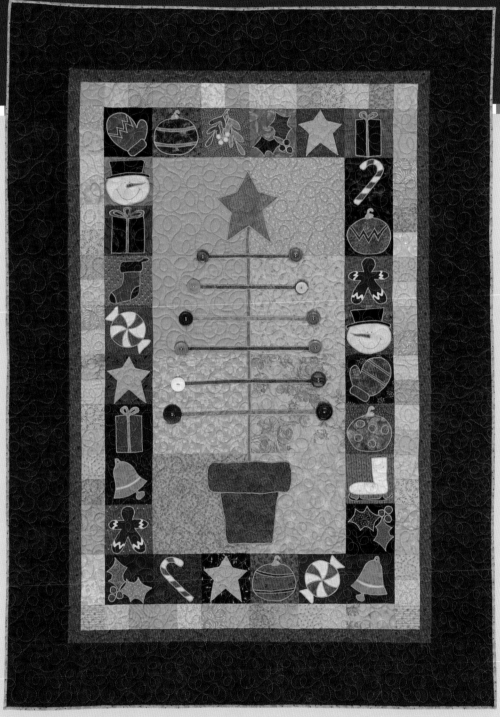

Charm your holiday guests by making it an old-fashioned Christmas with this button tree wall quilt. The quilt features appliqué along with very simple piecing. *Quilted by Lynn Helmke*

Finished Wall Quilt: 40½″ × 56½″

✳ Materials

2 yards total assorted tans for pieced appliqué background and pieced border

1¼ yards total assorted darks for appliqué border backgrounds and appliqué pieces

½ yard total assorted lights for appliqué pieces

1⅓ yards red print for accent border

1½ yards dark green for outer border

3½ yards for backing

½ yard for binding

2½ yards of paper-backed fusible web

12 buttons

✳ Cutting

✳ From the assorted tans:

Cut 8 squares 8½″ × 8½″ for the pieced appliqué background.

Cut 68 squares 2½″ × 2½″ for the pieced border.

✳ Cut 28 squares 4½″ × 4½″ from the assorted darks for the appliqué border backgrounds.

✳ Pieced Background

1. Sew together 2 rows of 4 tan squares 8½″ × 8½″ for the pieced background.

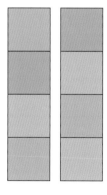

Piece center.

2. Join the rows, forming a large rectangle.

✳ Appliqué Tree

1. Cut the star and pot appliqué pieces (the patterns are on pages 61–62).

2. For the tree, cut strips ⅜″ by the following lengths: 20½″ for the trunk, and 8″, 9½″, 11″, 11½″, 12″, and 13″ for the branches.

3. Appliqué the appropriate pieces onto the background.

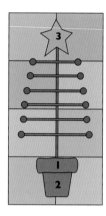

Appliqué tree.

✳ Appliqué Blocks

1. Cut the block appliqué pieces (the patterns are on pages 59–62).

2. Appliqué the appropriate pieces onto each border block.

  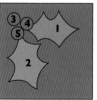

Block A, make 2. *Block B, make 1.* *Block C, make 3.*

  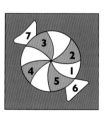

Block D, make 3. *Block E, make 1, and 1 reversed.* *Block F, make 2.*

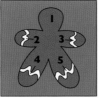

Block G, make 2. *Block H, make 1.* *Block I, make 2.*

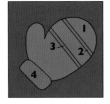
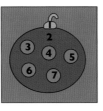

Block J, make 1, and 1 reversed. *Block K, make 1.* *Block L, make 1.*

Block M, make 1. *Block N, make 1, and 1 reversed.* *Block O, make 1.*

Block P, make 1. *Block Q, make 1.*

❄ Putting It All Together

Refer to the diagram at right.

BORDERS

Appliqué Border

1. Sew together 2 rows of 8 appliqué blocks for the side borders. Sew the borders to the quilt top. Press.

2. Sew together 2 rows of 6 appliqué blocks for the top and bottom borders. Sew the borders to the quilt top. Press.

Pieced Border

1. Sew together 2 rows of 20 tan squares $2\frac{1}{2}'' \times 2\frac{1}{2}''$ for the side borders. Sew the borders to the quilt top. Press.

2. Sew together 2 rows of 14 tan squares $2\frac{1}{2}'' \times 2\frac{1}{2}''$ for the top and bottom borders. Sew the borders to the quilt top. Press.

Accent Border

1. From the red print fabric, cut 2 strips $1\frac{1}{2}'' \times 44\frac{1}{2}''$ for the 2 side borders. Sew the borders to the quilt top. Press.

2. Cut 2 strips $1\frac{1}{2}'' \times 30\frac{1}{2}''$ for the top and bottom borders. Sew the borders to the quilt top. Press.

Outer Border

1. From the dark green fabric, cut 2 strips $5\frac{1}{2}'' \times 46\frac{1}{2}''$ for the 2 side borders. Sew the borders to the quilt top. Press.

2. Cut 2 strips $5\frac{1}{2}'' \times 40\frac{1}{2}''$ for the top and bottom borders. Sew the borders to the quilt top. Press.

FINISHING

1. Layer the quilt with batting and backing, and baste or pin.

2. Quilt as desired, and bind.

3. Sew the buttons in place at the ends of the branches.

Putting it all together

A warm gold and red pieced border frames these easy-to-appliqué star trees.

Quilted by Lynn Helmke

Finished Block size: 10″ × 10″

Finished Wall Quilt: 56½″ × 56½″

❋ Materials

2 yards total assorted tans for appliqué block backgrounds

1 yard total assorted greens for trees

¼ yard total assorted browns for tree trunks

2 yards total assorted golds for stars and pieced borders

¾ yard total assorted reds for pieced borders

4 yards for backing and binding

2½ yards of paper-backed fusible web

❋ Cutting

❋ Cut 16 squares 10½″ × 10½″ from the assorted tans for the appliqué block backgrounds.

❋ Cut 24 squares 5¼″ × 5¼″ from the assorted reds for the pieced borders. Cut the squares on the diagonal twice for a total of 96 triangles.

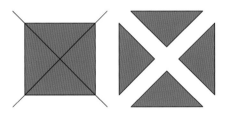

Cut squares on diagonal twice.

❋ Cut 96 squares 2⅞″ × 2⅞″ from the assorted golds for the pieced borders. Cut the squares on the diagonal for a total of 192 triangles.

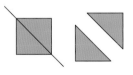

Cut squares on diagonal.

❋ Cut 88 rectangles 2½″ × 4½″ from the assorted golds for the pieced borders.

❋ Cut 4 squares 4½″ × 4½″ from the assorted golds for the pieced borders.

❋ Appliqué Blocks

1. Cut the star and tree appliqué pieces (the patterns are on Pullout 1, Side B, at the back of the book). Cut 16 each of Pattern 1, 2, and 3.

2. Appliqué the appropriate pieces onto the backgrounds.

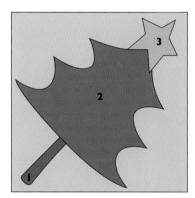

Make 16.

❋ Putting It All Together

Refer to the diagram on page 36.

BLOCKS

1. Arrange and sew together the appliqué blocks in 4 rows of 4 blocks each. Press.

2. Sew together the rows to form the quilt top. Press.

BORDERS

Inner Border

1. Sew 2 gold triangles to 1 red triangle on the diagonal edges. Make 40. Press.

Sew triangles, make 40.

2. Arrange and sew 4 rows of 10 blocks each to form the inner borders. Press.

3. Sew 2 gold triangles together on the diagonal edges to form a square for the corner units. Press. Make 4.

4. Sew the corner units to each end of the top and bottom borders. Press.

5. Sew the side borders to the quilt top. Press. Sew the top and bottom borders to the quilt top. Press.

Middle Border

1. Sew 4 rows of 22 gold rectangles to form the middle borders. Press.

2. Sew 1 gold square to each end of the top and bottom borders. Press.

3. Sew the side borders to the quilt top. Press. Sew the top and bottom borders to the quilt top. Press.

Outer Border

1. Sew 2 gold triangles to 1 red triangle on the diagonal edges. Refer to the diagram on page 35. Make 48 blocks. Press.

2. Arrange and sew 4 rows of 12 blocks each to form the outer borders. Press. Refer to the diagram at right.

3. Sew a gold triangle on each end of the border strips along the straight edges.

4. Sew the side borders to the quilt top. Press. Sew the top and bottom borders to the quilt top. Press.

5. Sew 2 red triangles together on the short edges for the corner units. Make 4. Press.

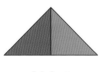

Make 4.

6. Sew the corner units to the quilt top. Press.

FINISHING

1. Layer the quilt top with batting and backing, and baste or pin.

2. Quilt as desired, and bind.

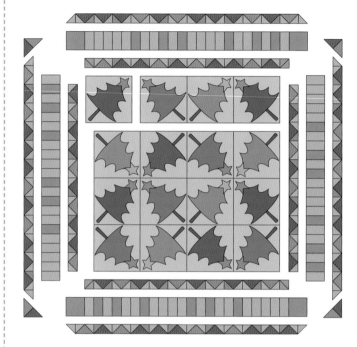

Putting it all together

Poinsettia Table Runner

Dress your holiday table with this rich, classic poinsettia runner. Fast and easy to complete, it will surely add warmth and charm to any décor. *Quilted by Lynn Helmke*

Finished Block Size: 8″ × 8″

Finished Table Runner: 20½″ × 44½″

❄ Materials

⅓ yard gold for appliqué block backgrounds

⅓ yard each 3 deep reds for poinsettias

⅛ yard bright red for poinsettias

⅛ yard or scrap of gold for poinsettia centers

½ yard total assorted tans and golds for inner border

¾ yard total assorted greens for outer border

1½ yards for backing

⅓ yard for binding

¾ yard of paper-backed fusible web

❄ Cutting

❈ Cut 3 squares 8½″ × 8½″ from the gold for the appliqué block backgrounds.

❈ Cut 12 rectangles 2½″ × 4½″ from the assorted tan and gold fabrics for the inner border.

❈ Cut 12 rectangles 2½″ × 6½″ from the assorted tan and gold fabrics for the inner border.

❈ Cut 28 squares 4½″ × 4½″ from the assorted greens for the outer border.

❄ Appliqué Blocks

1. Cut the poinsettia appliqué pieces (the patterns are on Pullout 1, Side B, at the back of the book). Cut 3 each of Patterns 1 through 13, and 9 of Pattern 14.

2. Appliqué the appropriate pieces onto the blocks. Make each block unique by varying the way the petals overlap each other.

Poinsettia block, make 3.

❄ Putting It All Together

Refer to the diagram on page 39.

PIECED BORDERS

Inner Border

1. Sew together 2 rectangles 2½″ × 4½″ from the assorted tans and golds on the short ends. Make 6 sets for the inner borders.

2. Sew together 2 rectangles 2½″ × 6½″ from the assorted tans and golds on the short ends. Make 6 sets for the inner borders.

3. Sew the inner borders to the appliqué blocks.

Piece inner borders.

4. Sew the appliquéd and bordered blocks together. Press.

Outer Border

1. Sew together 2 rows of 9 squares from the assorted greens for the side borders. Sew them to the table runner. Press.

2. Sew together 2 rows of 5 squares from the assorted greens for the top and bottom borders. Sew them to the table runner. Press.

FINISHING

1. Layer the table runner with batting and backing, and baste or pin.

2. Quilt as desired, and bind.

Putting it all together

Bring a cozy, warm feel to your holiday décor with this easily pieced and fusible-appliquéd table runner.

Quilted by Lynn Helmke

Finished Table Runner: 20½" × 40½"

❄ Materials

⅝ yard total assorted golds for pieced center

⅓ yard total assorted greens for trees

⅛ yard gold for stars

¾ yard total assorted darks for pieced border

1¼ yards for backing

⅓ yard for binding

⅔ yard of paper-backed fusible web

❄ Cutting

❄ Cut 24 squares 4½″ × 4½″ from the assorted golds for the pieced center.

❄ Cut 52 rectangles 2½″ × 4½″ from the assorted darks for the pieced borders.

❄ Pieced Background

1. Sew 3 rows of 8 squares each from the assorted golds for the pieced center.

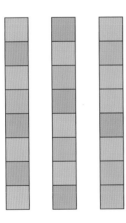

Piece center.

2. Sew together the 3 rows, forming a large rectangle.

❄ Appliqué

1. Cut the star and trees appliqué pieces (the patterns are on Pullout 1, Side A, at the back of the book). Cut 4 each of Patterns 1 and 2. Cut 2 each of Patterns 3 and 4.

2. Appliqué the appropriate pieces onto the background using the diagram below.

❄ Putting It All Together

Refer to the diagram below.

BORDER

1. Sew together 2 rows of 16 rectangles from the assorted darks for the side borders. Sew the borders to the background, and press toward the borders.

2. Sew together 2 rows of 10 rectangles from the assorted darks for the top and bottom borders. Sew the borders to the background, and press toward the borders.

FINISHING

1. Layer the table runner top with batting and backing, and baste or pin.

2. Quilt as desired, and bind.

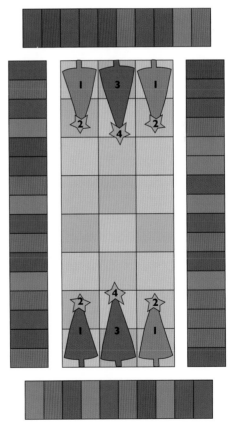

Putting it all together

Holly Berry Table Topper

 Dress up your holiday table with this simple, yet elegant, table topper. *Quilted by Lynn Helmke*

Finished Table Topper: 36½″ × 36½″

❄ Materials

1¼ yards total assorted tans for appliqué background

1½ yards total assorted greens for pieced center, holly leaves, and outer border

⅛ yard total assorted reds for berries

1¼ yards for backing

⅓ yard for binding

1½ yards of paper-backed fusible web

❄ Cutting

❄ Cut 48 squares 4½″ × 4½″ from the assorted tans for the appliqué background.

❄ Cut 16 squares 4½″ × 4½″ from the assorted greens for the pieced center.

❄ Cut 68 squares 2½″ × 2½″ from the assorted greens for the outer border.

❄ Piecing

1. Sew together 4 rows of 4 squares 4½″ × 4½″ from the assorted greens. Sew the rows together to form the pieced center. Press.

Piece center.

2. Sew together 2 rows of 4 squares 4½″ × 4½″ from the assorted tans for the appliqué background. Make 2. Press.

3. Sew together 2 rows of 8 squares 4½″ × 4½″ from the assorted tans for the appliqué background. Make 2. Press.

4. Sew the appliqué backgrounds to the pieced center. Press.

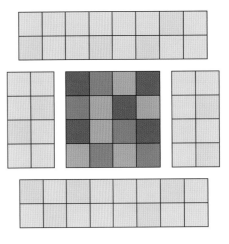

Piecing layout

❄ Appliqué

1. Use the holly and berry vine patterns (the patterns are on Pullout 1, Side A, at the back of the book) to cut:

❄ 4 of Pattern 1

❄ 24 of Pattern 2

❄ 16 of Pattern 3

❄ 8 of Pattern 4

2. Appliqué the appropriate pieces onto the background.

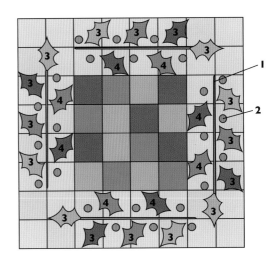

Appliqué layout

❄ Putting It All Together

Refer to the diagram at right.

OUTER BORDER

1. Sew together 2 rows of 16 squares 2½″ × 2½″ from the assorted greens for the side borders. Sew the borders to the table topper.

2. Sew together 2 rows of 18 squares 2½″ × 2½″ from the assorted greens for the top and bottom borders. Sew the borders to the table topper.

FINISHING

1. Layer the top with batting and backing, and baste or pin.

2. Quilt as desired, and bind.

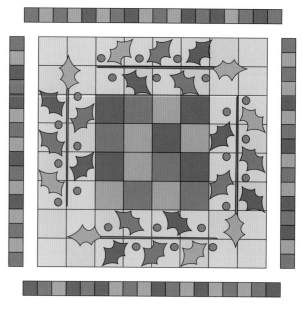

Putting it all together

Mini Tree Skirts

PIECED MINI TREE SKIRT

Your tree will be skirted in style with this easy-to-make mini tree skirt. It's a great way to use leftover Christmas fabric scraps. This tree skirt is a perfect size for a tabletop tree.

Finished Tree Skirt: 18″ diameter

❄ Materials

1¼ yards total assorted Christmas fabrics

1 yard for backing and binding

Template plastic

❄ Cutting

1. Make a plastic template of Pattern 1 (on Pullout 1, Side A, at the back of the book).

2. Cut 72 rectangles 1½″ × 9″ from the assorted Christmas fabrics.

❄ Piecing

1. Sew together in random order 9 rectangles 1½″ × 9″ to form a block. Press flat. Make 8 blocks.

Piece blocks, make 8.

2. Place the plastic template on top of the block at an angle. Trace around the template. Cut on the line. Make 8 skirt segments, varying the angle of the template placement for each block.

Trace around template.

❄ Putting It All Together

Refer to the diagram below.

SKIRT SEGMENTS

Arrange and sew the pieces together along the straight edges. Leave 2 edges open for the tree skirt opening.

FINISHING

1. Layer the tree skirt with batting and backing, and baste or pin.

2. Quilt as desired, and bind with bias binding.

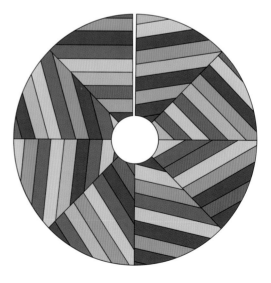

Putting it all together

HOLLY BERRY MINI TREE SKIRT

Holly leaves and berry vines adorn this appliquéd mini tree skirt. At 18″ in diameter, this tree skirt is a perfect fit for a mini tree.

Finished Tree Skirt: 18″ diameter

❄ Materials

¼ yard each 8 reds for appliqué backgrounds

⅛ yard total assorted lights for berries

⅛ yard black for vines

⅛ yard total assorted greens for holly leaves

1 yard for backing and binding

½ yard of paper-backed fusible web

Template plastic

❄ Cutting

1. Make a plastic template of Pattern 1 (on Pullout 1, Side A, at the back of the book).

2. Cut 8 of Pattern 1 from the assorted red fabrics for appliqué backgrounds.

❄ Appliqué

1. Cut the holly and berry appliqué pieces (the patterns are on Pullout 1, Side A, at the back of the book). Cut 8 each of Patterns 1 through 6.

2. Appliqué the appropriate pieces onto the background.

Appliqué tree skirt sections, make 8.

❄ Putting It All Together

Refer to the diagram below.

SKIRT SEGMENTS

Arrange and sew the pieces together along the straight edges. Leave 2 edges open for the tree skirt opening.

FINISHING

1. Layer the tree skirt with batting and backing, and baste or pin.

2. Quilt as desired, and bind with bias binding.

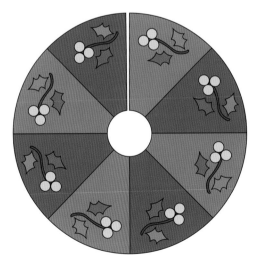

Putting it all together

Holiday Coasters

Spread the holiday spirit throughout the house with these easy-to-make woolfelt holiday coasters. What a great gift giving idea!

Finished Coaster: 4″

❄ Materials

For each set of 9 coasters:

⅓ yard total woolfelt for coasters

⅛ yard each or scraps of woolfelt for appliqué backgrounds

⅛ yard each or scraps of various colors of woolfelt for appliqué pieces

½ yard of paper-backed fusible web

Permanent markers for faces

❄ Cutting

Cut 2 of Pattern 1 for each coaster. Cut 1 of Pattern 2 for appliqué backgrounds for each coaster (the patterns are on page 58).

❄ Appliqué

1. Cut the appliqué pieces (the patterns are on pages 57–58).

2. Appliqué the appropriate pieces onto each coaster background circle, using a zigzag or satin stitch.

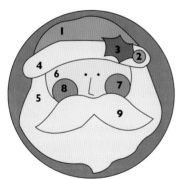

Santa coaster layout

Tree coaster layout

Poinsettia coaster layout

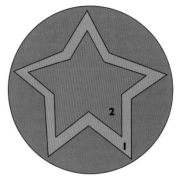

Star coaster layout

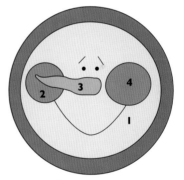

Snowman coaster layout

Ornament coaster layout

Candy cane coaster layout

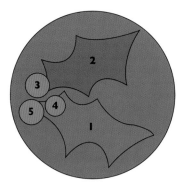

Holly berry coaster layout

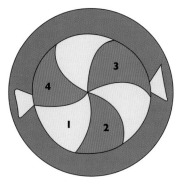

Peppermint coaster layout

❄ Putting It All Together

COASTERS

1. Layer 2 large circles (Pattern 1) one on top of the other. Sew the circles together along the outside edge using a zigzag or satin stitch.

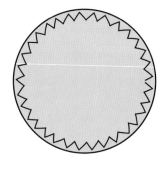

Sew circles together.

2. Center the background on the coaster. Sew the background circle onto the coaster through all the layers along the outside edge using a zigzag or satin stitch.

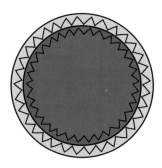

Sew background to coaster.

FINISHING

Draw faces on the snowman and Santa coasters using a permanent marker.

Delight the sports enthusiast in your family with one of these sport-savvy Santas. Use a purchased towel, or make your own with homespun fabrics.

Finished Towel: 19″ × 29″

❄ Materials

For each towel:

¾ yard homespun plaid or checked fabric for towel

⅛ yard each or scraps of various fabrics for appliqué pieces

¼ yard of paper-backed fusible web

Black and red permanent markers for faces and other details

❄ Towel

1. To make the towel, cut the homespun 21″ × 31″.

2. Turn under the edges ½″ on the sides of the towel, and press. Turn under the sides another ½″, and press.

3. Sew ⅛″ from the folded edge on both sides. Repeat for the top and bottom edges of the towel.

Ready-made towels are also available at your local quilt shop or department store.

❄ Appliqué

1. Cut the appliqué pieces (the patterns are on Pullout 3, Side B, at the back of the book).

2. Appliqué the appropriate pieces onto each towel using a zigzag or satin stitch.

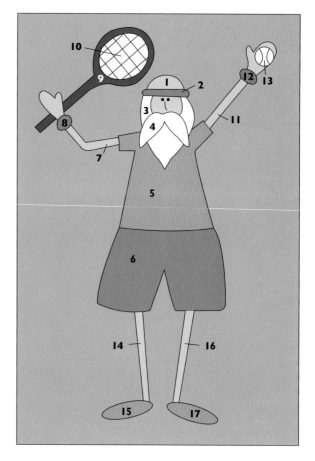

Tennis Santa layout

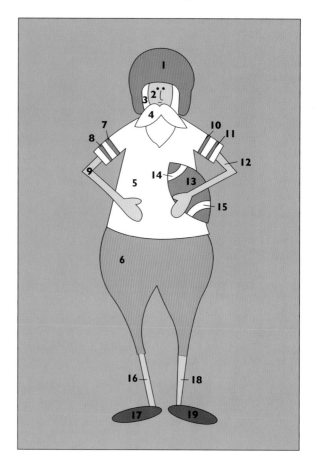

Football Santa layout

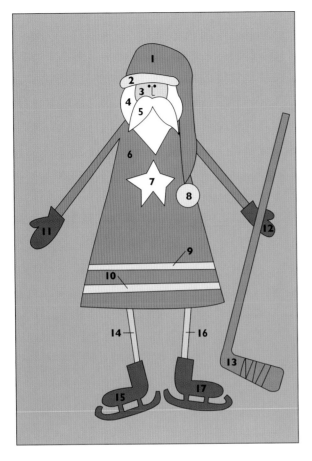

Hockey Santa layout

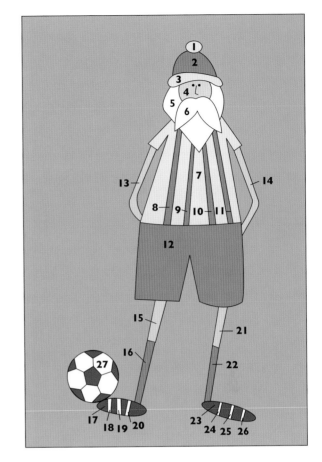

Soccer Santa layout

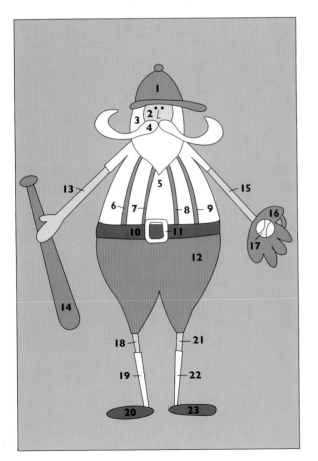

Baseball Santa layout

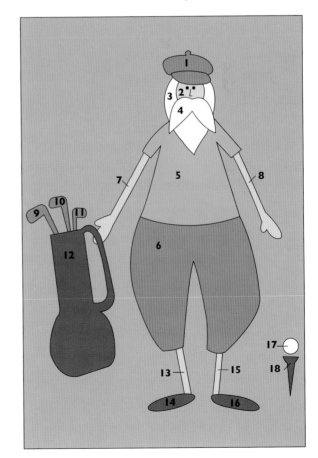

Golf Santa layout

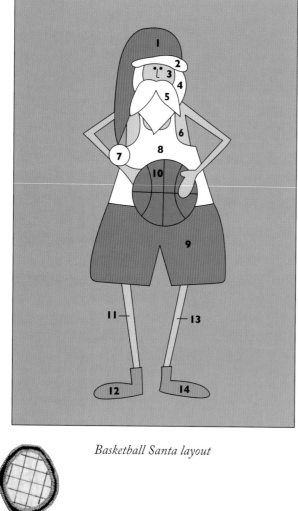

Basketball Santa layout

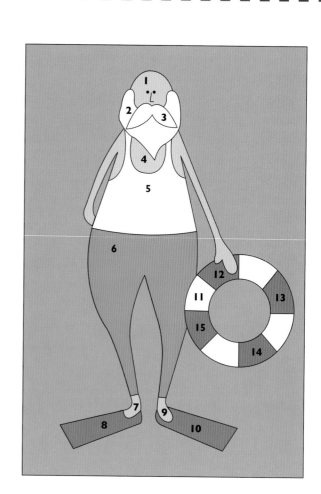

Swimming Santa layout

❄ Finishing

Use the permanent markers to draw Santa's face and other details as needed.

A Cozy Quilted Christmas

Button Tree Topiaries

Got buttons? So do I. I love buttons and have collected them for years. These topiaries are a great way to show off some favorites. I used buttons in whites, ivories, and tans. Change the look by using multicolored buttons, all red buttons, all gold buttons, and so on.

Finished Small Tree: 21″

Finished Medium Tree: 26″

Finished Large Tree: 30″

❄ Materials

	SMALL	MEDIUM	LARGE
GREEN WOOLFELT	¹/₃ yard	¹/₂ yard	³/₄ yard
BUTTONS	75	120	188
STRAIGHT STICK	18″ long, ¹/₂″ diameter	23″ long, ³/₄″ diameter	27″ long, 1″ diameter
CLAY POT	4″	5″	6″

For each tree you will also need:

* ❄ Polyester fiberfill
* ❄ Styrofoam for inside clay pot
* ❄ Hot-glue gun
* ❄ Hot glue sticks
* ❄ Spanish moss
* ❄ Raffia for bow

❄ Cutting

Cut 2 of Pattern 1 and 1 of Pattern 2 for each tree (the patterns are on Pullout 3, Side B, at the back of the book).

❄ Putting It All Together

1. Arrange and sew buttons on 1 side of each Pattern 1, being careful to stay at least ¹/₂″ away from all edges.

2. Sew the trees, wrong sides together, ¹/₄″ from the edges along the long sides. I used a straight stitch on the machine, but you could also blanket stitch by hand. The raw edges will show.

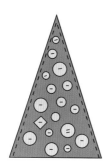

Sew together sides of trees.

3. Stuff the tip of the tree with fiberfill. Insert the stick into the center of the tree, and continue stuffing the tree with fiberfill. Be sure to stuff evenly around the stick to keep it centered.

4. Cut an opening in Pattern 2 along the dotted line. You may need to adjust the size slightly, depending on the diameter of your stick. The opening should be just big enough for the stick to fit through snugly.

5. Place the stick through the opening, and gently slide the bottom piece up to meet the edges of the tree. Adjust the piece, and hand stitch onto the bottom edge of the tree.

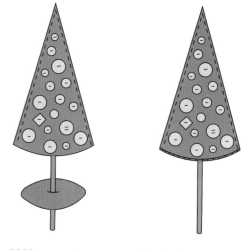

Add bottom piece.   *Hand stitch tree bottom.*

6. Fill the clay pot with Styrofoam to within 1″ of the top. You may need to trim the Styrofoam to fit.

7. Push the bottom of the tree trunk stick through the center of the Styrofoam to the bottom of the pot. Hot glue around the inside of the pot to keep the Styrofoam firmly in place.

8. Arrange and hot glue the Spanish moss to the Styrofoam.

9. Tie the raffia bow onto the tree.

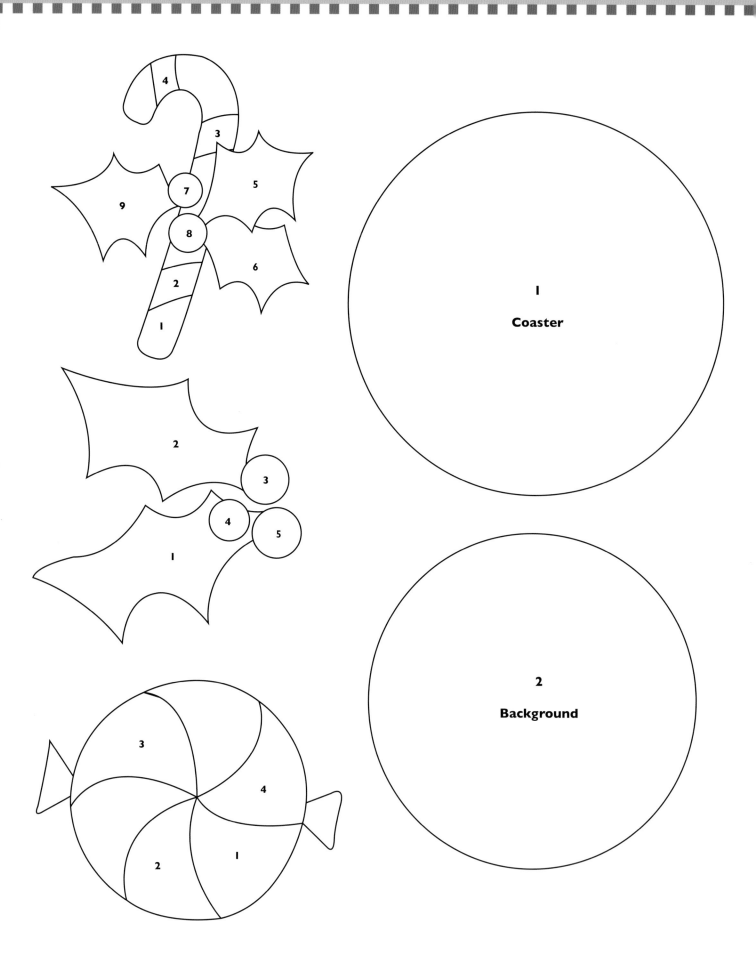

❄ O Christmas Tree Patterns

A Cozy Quilted Christmas

J

I

2

3

L

I

2

3

4

5

6

7

G

2

I

K I

2

3

4

3

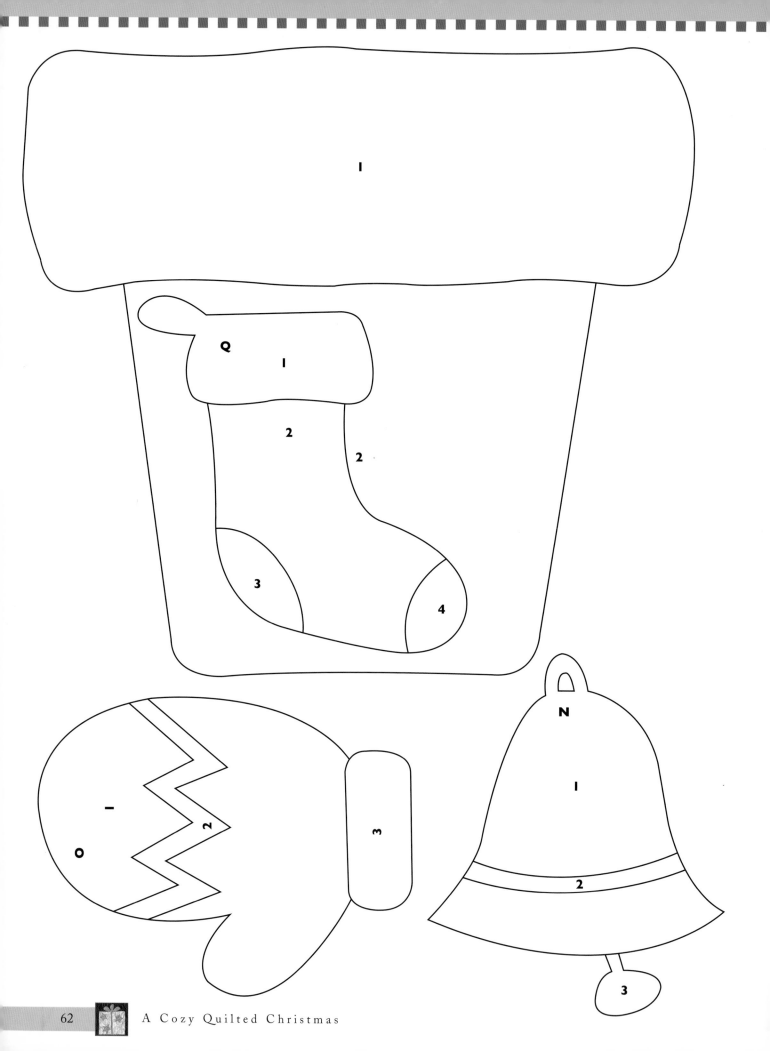

A Cozy Quilted Christmas

About the Author

Kim Schaefer is from southeastern Wisconsin, where she lives with her husband, Gary; her sons, Max, Ben, Sam, and Gator; and her dog, Rio—all of whom she lovingly refers to as the "Neanderthals." Kim and Gary also have two daughters, Cody and Ali. Cody lives nearby, and Ali attends college in Minnesota. Kim's stepsons, Gary Jr. and Dax, also live nearby, and her stepdaughters, Tina and Danielle, live in Phoenix.

Kim began sewing at an early age, which, according to Kim, was a nightmare for her mom, who continually and patiently untangled bobbin messes. Kim was formally educated at the University of Wisconsin in Milwaukee, where she studied fine arts and majored in fibers. At age 23, Kim took her first quilting class and was immediately hooked.

In 1996, Little Country Quilts was born and made its debut at Quilt Market in Minneapolis. In addition to designing quilt patterns, Kim designs fabric for Andover/Makower and works with Leo Licensing, which licenses her designs for nonfabric products.

Also by Kim Schaefer

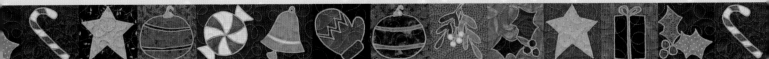

Quilting Supplies

Cotton Patch Mail Order

3404 Hall Lane

Dept. CTB

Lafayette, CA 94549

800-835-4418; 925-283-7883

email: quiltusa@yahoo.com

website: www.quiltusa.com

Note: Fabrics used in the projects shown may not be currently available; fabric manufacturers keep most fabrics in print for only a short time.